The Epistles of
HEBREWS
& JAMES

THE MORNINGSTAR VISION BIBLE

by Rick Joyner

MorningStar Publications

The Epistles of Hebrews & James, The MorningStar Vision Bible
by Rick Joyner
Copyright ©2014
Trade Size Edition

Distributed by MorningStar Publications, Inc.,
a division of MorningStar Fellowship Church
375 Star Light Drive, Fort Mill, SC 29715

www.MorningStarMinistries.org
1-800-542-0278

Cover and Layout Design: Kevin Lepp and Kandi Evans

ISBN— 978-1-60708-567-6; 1-60708-567-4

For a free catalog of MorningStar Resources, please call 1-800-542-0278

The Epistles of Hebrews & James
TABLE OF CONTENTS

PREFACE
THE MORNINGSTAR VISION BIBLE
BY RICK JOYNER

Next to His Son and the Holy Spirit, The Bible is God's greatest gift to mankind. What treasure on earth could be compared to one Word from God? There is good reason why The Bible is the bestselling book of all time by such a wide margin. The importance of The Bible cannot be overstated. If Jesus, who is the Word, would take His stand on the written Word when challenged by the devil, how much more must we be established on that Word to take our stand and live our lives by it?

The most basic purpose of **The MorningStar Vision Bible** is accuracy and faithfulness to the intended meaning of the Author, the Holy Spirit. His written Word reveals the path to life, salvation, transformation, deliverance, and healing for every soul who would seek to know God. The universe is upheld by the Word of His power, so there is no stronger foundation that we could ever build our lives on other than His Word. Therefore, we have pursued this project with the utmost care in that what is presented here is His Word and not ours. We were very careful not to let anyone work on it that had an agenda other than a love for the truth and the deepest respect for the fact that we were handling this most precious treasure—God's own Word.

The primary accuracy of any translation is its adherence to the original text in the original languages The Bible was written in, Hebrew and Greek. However, there are problems when you try to translate from a language such as Greek into a language like English because Greek is so much more expressive than English. For example, there are several different Greek words with different meanings that are translated as one word "love" in our English version. The Greek words distinguish between such things as friendship love, erotic attraction, or unconditional love. When we just translate these as "love," it may be generally true, but something basic in what the Author tried to convey is left out. As we mature in Christ by following the Spirit, these deeper, more specific meanings become important. Therefore, we have sought to include the nuances of the Greek language in this version.

A basic biblical guide we used for this work was Psalm 12:6: **"The words of the LORD are pure words; as silver tried in a furnace on the earth, refined seven times."** Every Book we release of this version has been through a meticulous process at least seven times to ensure faithfulness to the original intent. Even so, we do not yet consider this to be a completed work. We are releasing these Book by Book in softcover to seek even further examination by those who read them. We are asking our readers to send us challenges for any word, phrase, or part that you think may not be accurate, along with your reasons. These will be received, considered, and researched with openness. If you have insights that you think should be added to the commentary, we will consider those as well.

You can email these or any comments that you have to bible@morningstarministries.org, or mail them to us at:

MorningStar Publications
375 Star Light Drive
Fort Mill, South Carolina 29715

Please include any credentials that you might have that would be relevant, but they are not necessary for this.

My personal credentials for compiling and editing such a work are first my love for The Bible and my respect for its integrity. I have been a Christian for more than forty years, and I have read The Bible through from cover to cover at least once a year. I do have an earned doctorate in theology from a good, accredited school, but have not used the title because I want my message received on the merits of its content, not by a title. Though I have been in pursuit of knowing the Lord and His Word for more than forty years, I still feel more comfortable thinking of myself as a student rather than an expert. If that bothers you I understand. But when handling the greatest truth the world has ever known, I feel we must be as humble and transparent as possible.

Most of those who have worked on this project with me have been students at MorningStar University. This is a unique school that has had students from ages sixteen to over eighty. Some have been remarkably skilled in languages, especially Hebrew and Greek. Some have been believers and students of the Word for a long time. Others were fairly new to the faith, but were strong and devoted to seeking and knowing the truth. These were the ones that I was especially interested in recruiting for this project because of the Lord's statement in Matthew 11:25:

> **At that time Jesus answered and said, "I praise You, O Father, Lord of heaven and earth, that You did hide these things from the wise and intelligent and did reveal them to babes."**

Because **"God resists the proud, but gives grace to the humble" (see James 4:6; I Peter 5:5 NKJV)**, the humility of a relatively young believer can be more important for discerning truth than great knowledge and experience if these have caused us to become proud.

Also, as Peter stated concerning Paul's writings in II Peter 3:15-16:

> **Paul, according to the wisdom given him, wrote to you,**
>
> **as also in all his letters, speaking in them of these things, in which are some things hard to understand, which the untaught and unstable distort, as they do also the rest of the Scriptures, to their own destruction.**

So the untaught can be prone to distort the truth if they are also unstable. This is why the relatively young believers that I sought to be a part of our team were not just stable but strong in the Lord and their resolve to know the truth.

Even so, not everyone who has great knowledge and experience has become so proud that it causes God to resist them. Those who have matured and yet remained humble and teachable may be some of the greatest treasures we have in the body of Christ. Such elders are certainly worthy of great honor and should be listened to and heeded. Nowhere in Scripture are we exhorted to honor the youth, but over and over we are commanded to honor the elders.

So it seems we have a paradox—the Lord reveals His ways to babes, but elders are the ones responsible for keeping His people on the path of life, walking in His ways. This is not a contradiction. As with many of the paradoxes in Scripture, the tension between the extremes is intended to help keep us on the path of life by giving us boundaries. Pride in our experience and knowledge can cause us to stray from this path, as can our lack of knowledge if it is combined with instability. The vision and exuberance of youth are needed to keep the fire of passion for the Lord and His ways burning. This is why the Lord said that the wise brought forth from their treasures things both new and old (see Matthew 13:52).

For this reason, I sought the young in the faith who are also stable and displayed a discipline and devotion to obedience to the truth. I also sought the contributions of the experienced and learned who continued to have the humility to whom God gives His grace. As far as Greek and Hebrew scholars, I was more interested in those who are technically-minded, devoted to details, and who seemed to be free of doctrinal prejudices.

This is not to give the impression that all who worked on this project went over the entire Bible. I did have some who went over the entire New Testament, but most only worked on a single Book, and sometimes just a single issue. I may not have told many of the Greek and Hebrew experts that it was for this project when I inquired about a matter with them.

I realize that this is a unique way to develop a Bible version, but as we are told in I Corinthians 13:12 we "see in part" and **"know in part."** Therefore, we all need to put what we have together with what others have if we are going to have a complete picture. This version is the result of many years of labor by many people. Having been a publisher for many years, I know every editor or proofreader will tend to catch different things, and so it has been with this project. We also realize that as hard as we have worked on being as accurate as possible, we may have missed some things, and we will be genuinely appreciative of every one that is caught by our readers. Again, our goal is to have the most accurate English version of The Bible possible.

Even though accuracy and faithfulness to the original intent of the Holy Spirit were our most basic devotions, we also sought insights that could come from many other factors, such as the culture of the times in which the different Books of The Bible were written. Along with myself, many other contributors have spent countless hours of research examining words, phrases, the authors of the Books of The Bible, their times, and even the history of cities and places mentioned in it. Though the knowledge gained by this research did not affect the words in the text of The Bible, they sometimes gave a greater illumination and depth to their meaning that was profound. Sometimes they made obscure, hard to comprehend phrases come to life.

One of the obvious intents of the Author was to be able to communicate to any seeker of truth on the level they are on. For the most basic seeker, knowing such things as the nuances or more detailed meaning of the Greek or Hebrew words may not be important. As we mature, we will seek deeper understanding if we follow the Holy Spirit. We are told in I Corinthians 2:10, **"For to us God revealed them through the Spirit; for the Spirit searches all things, even the depths of God."** Therefore, those who follow the Spirit will not be shallow in their understanding of anything and will especially search to know the depths of the nature of God.

Our single greatest hope is that **The MorningStar Vision Bible** will accurately reveal the will and intent of the Lord and compel all who read it to love Him more, which is our highest purpose of man. If we love Him more, we will then begin to love one another more. As we grow in love, we will also grow in our devotion to know Him even more, know His ways, and do the things that please Him. He deserves this from us more than could ever be expressed.

There is nothing greater than knowing Him. I am convinced that anything we learn about God will make us love Him more, which is our chief purpose and the one thing that will determine if we are successful human beings. This is also the only thing that can lead to the true peace and true joy that is beyond anything this world can supply. There is no greater adventure that can be had in this life than the true Christian life. The Bible is the map to the greatest quest and the greatest adventure that we could ever experience.

INTRODUCTION
THE EPISTLE TO THE HEBREWS

Of all the Epistles in the New Testament, Hebrews is unique and is considered the deepest theologically. It is also one of the most important for fortifying the New Covenant we have in Christ. It is addressed to the Jewish people about their greatest hope, the Messiah, engaging in an in-depth overview of how the Old Covenant law prophesied Christ and was fulfilled in Him.

The first five chapters of this great letter could make a comprehensive course in Christology in any seminary. They beautifully and powerfully establish that Jesus is the Messiah and also the Creator through whom the world was made, conveying the glory, majesty, and preeminence He has as the Son of God. This is addressed in other places such as chapter one of the Gospel of John, but not with the depth and scope found in these first chapters of Hebrews.

Added to this is the recognition of Jesus as the High Priest of the New Covenant. This transcendent teaching about Christ includes the unfathomable calling to be His brethren, not just His subjects. These who follow Him are also called to serve with Him as priests after the order of Melchizedek, which is introduced here.

Next an overview of the Old Covenant priesthood is given and what it accomplished. Then this is overlaid by contrasting how much more is accomplished by the New Covenant priesthood established by Christ and His atonement sacrifice. The Old Covenant priesthood was a prophetic model, but we now serve as priests of the fulfillment. Here we are given the instructions of how we serve.

This remarkable Epistle then concludes with one of the greatest exhortations on faith, found in chapter eleven, calling us to follow in the footsteps of all who have lived and walked by faith in service of our God. In chapter twelve, we are exhorted to appreciate the discipline we endure because of God's love for us and to stand firm in the great shaking of all things by standing on the only ground that cannot be shaken—the kingdom. Finally the Epistle ends with one of the most powerful and succinct calls to walk in practical Christianity, loving and honoring God and His people.

All of the works included in the canon of Scripture were subjected to the most vigorous tests of authenticity and consistency with the apostolic doctrine. In virtually every way it could be tested, this Epistle to the Hebrews scored the highest and had little challenge to taking its rightful place in the canon. Notwithstanding, the authorship of this Epistle is still often and widely debated.

Because of its style, vocabulary, and other internal and external evidence, most believe the author was the Apostle Paul. Others consider that its author could have been one of Paul's companions in the work, such as Silas, Luke, Barnabas, or Apollos. Others have attributed it to Clement of Rome or some unknown Alexandrian Christian. Even though its authorship is still ambiguous, the sound teaching, scope, and depth of the Epistle make it one of the pillars of true apostolic Christianity.

Those who accept Paul as the author of Hebrews believe it was penned near the end of his two-year imprisonment in Rome. Almost all believe that it was written before 70 A.D. and the destruction of Jerusalem, since this event would have certainly been mentioned in such a letter to the Jewish people had it occurred.

THE EPISTLE TO THE
HEBREWS

Hebrews 1

The Preeminence of the Son

1   God, having spoken to the fathers by the prophets at many times and in many ways from ancient times,

2   has in these last days spoken to us by His Son, whom He appointed the heir of all things, through whom also He created the world.

3   Who, being the fullness of His glory and the very image of His essence, and upholding all things by the word of His power, when He had made purification for sin, sat down at the right hand of the Majesty on high.

4   He has become so much greater than the angels, as He has inherited a more excellent name than they.

5   For to which of the angels did He say at any time, "You are My Son. This day have I begotten You?" (see Psalm 2:7) And again, "I will be a Father to Him, and He will be a Son to Me?" (see II Samuel 7:14)

6   When He again brings the Firstborn into the world He says, "Let all the angels of God worship Him" (see Psalm 97:7).

7   Of the angels He said, "Who makes His angels winds, and His ministers a flame a fire" (see Psalm 104:4).

8   but of the Son He says, "Your throne, O God, is forever and ever, and the scepter of righteousness is the scepter of Your kingdom.

9   "You have loved righteousness, and hated iniquity; therefore God, Your God has anointed You with the oil of gladness above Your brethren" (see Psalm 45:6-7).

10 "You, Lord, in the beginning did lay the foundation of the earth, and the heavens are the works of Your hands.

11 "They will perish, but You will continue, and they all will become old like a garment,

12 "and as a mantle You will roll them up. Like a garment they will be changed. But You are the same, and Your times shall not come to an end" (see Psalm 102:25-26).

13 Of which of the angels has He said at any time, "Sit at My right hand until I make Your enemies a footstool for Your feet?" (see Psalm 110:1)

14 Are they not all ministering spirits, sent forth to serve the ones who will inherit salvation?

The Preeminence of the Son

Hebrews 1:1-14: This Epistle gives an overview of the whole plan of God from beginning to end. It starts with the foundation of all things—the position and preeminence of the Son of God. This is the basic revelation of the purpose of creation and the truth upon which all other truth stands.

As we are told here, Jesus is the Creator, the one who laid the foundation for creation of the physical world and is over all of creation in both heaven and earth. Therefore, He should also be the preeminent devotion of every one who seeks God, as no one can come to the Father except through the Son. The purposes of God cannot be understood apart from the Son. As we are told in Ephesians 1, all things will be summed up in the Son—He is the ultimate purpose of God. If we do not keep our attention focused on the ultimate purpose of God—growing up in all things into Him—we will be in danger of being distracted by the lesser purposes of God. Every other truth, every other purpose, serves this one.

Jesus is the River of Life. All other truths and purposes of God are but tributaries that flow into Him. We must not be distracted from the River of Life by the tributaries that flow into it. Every doctrine and every other purpose will lead to

Christ if it is true. The Epistle begins by fortifying this basic and ultimate truth, declaring that this ultimate purpose of God is the ultimate purpose of every Christian. How are we summing up everything in our lives in Him?

1:9: In this verse, we are told that it was because Jesus loved righteousness and hated wickedness that He received the "oil of joy." The joy of the Lord is linked to loving righteousness and hating wickedness. Even so, as we see demonstrated by the life of Christ, who had no tolerance for self-righteousness and was "a friend of sinners," self-righteousness can be the worst wickedness. Sinners who come to Jesus are made righteous by Him.

NOTES

The Epistle to the
HEBREWS
Hebrews 2

Called to Be His Brethren

1 Therefore we should give even more earnest heed to the things that we have heard, lest in any way we should drift away from them.

2 For if the word spoken through angels proved sure, and every transgression and disobedience of them received a just recompense,

3 how then will we escape if we neglect so great a salvation that, having at the first been spoken through the Lord, was confirmed to us by those who heard?

4 God also bears witness to them both by signs and wonders, with many works of power, and by the gifts of the Holy Spirit, according to His own will.

5 For it was not to angels that He subjected the age to come of which we speak.

6 One somewhere has testified, saying, "What is man that You are mindful of him? Or the son of man, that You visit him?

7 "You made him a little lower than the angels, but You crowned him with glory and honor, and set him over the works of Your hands:

8 "You did put all things in subjection, under his feet" (see Psalm 8:4-6). By the fact that He subjected all things to Him, He left nothing that is not subject to Him. However, now we do not see all things subjected to Him,

9 but we see Him who was for a time made a little lower than the angels, even Jesus, because of the suffering of death He is crowned

with glory and honor. It was by the grace of God He should taste of death for every man.

10 It became Him, for whom all things were made, and through whom are all things made, and Who will bring many sons to glory, to perfect the Author of their salvation through sufferings.

11 For both He that sanctifies, and those who are sanctified, are all one. For this reason He is not ashamed to call them brethren,

12 saying, "I will declare Your name to My brethren. In the midst of the congregation will I sing Your praise" (see Psalm 22:22).

13 Again we read, "I will put my trust in Him." Then, "Behold, I and the children whom God has given to Me" (see Isaiah 8:17-18).

14 Since the children are partakers in flesh and blood, He also in like manner partook of the same so that through death He might bring to an end him that had the power of death, that is, the devil.

15 By this He delivered those who through fear of death were subject to bondage their entire lives.

16 For it was not to angels that He gives help, but He gives help to the seed of Abraham.

17 Therefore it behooved Him in all things to be made like His brethren, that He might become a merciful and faithful High Priest in things pertaining to God, and to make propitiation for the sins of the people.

18 For in that He too has Himself suffered temptation He is able to help those that are tempted.

Called to Be His Brethren

Hebrews 2:1-18: Here, the declaration of the preeminence of Jesus as the main purpose of God is continued with the reason for His sufferings. He could have been executed, satisfying the requirements for the atonement without torture and pain. Yet He went as far as He could to identify with the suffering of mankind, to fully feel what we feel. This is a love and majesty beyond comprehension, and we will forever be worshipping Him for it.

This is also one of the key discourses in Scripture about the reason the righteous are allowed to suffer. The apostles prayed after they had been beaten, thanking God to have been allowed to suffer shame for His name's sake. This is one of the greatest honors we can have on this earth. It is one way that we grow in character, to be like the One who suffered more unjustly than anyone ever will. Even so, more than being about what we get out of this honor, it is one of the primary ways that the basic and powerful truth of the gospel is demonstrated by those who love the truth. We are called to love the same way He did, and He loved us more than He loved His own life.

NOTES

THE EPISTLE TO THE
HEBREWS

Hebrews 3

Consider Jesus

1 Therefore, holy brethren, partakers of a heavenly calling, consider Jesus, the Apostle and High Priest of our confession,

2 who was faithful to Him who appointed Him as also Moses was in his house.

3 For He has been counted worthy of more glory than Moses, just as He that built the house has more honor than the house.

4 For every house is built by someone, but He that built all things is God.

5 Moses was indeed faithful in his house as a servant, for a testimony of those things that were to be revealed later,

6 but Christ, was faithful as a Son over His house, whose house we are if we hold fast our confession with boldness and the glory of our hope firm to the end.

7 Therefore, even as the Holy Spirit says, "Today if you will hear His voice,

8 "do not harden your hearts as in the day of provocation, like the day of the trial in the wilderness,

9 "where your fathers tried Me by testing Me, and saw My works for forty years.

10 "Therefore I was displeased with that generation, and said, 'They always go astray in their heart, and they did not know My ways.

11 'As I swore in My wrath, they will not enter My rest'" (see Psalm 95:7-11).

12 Take heed, brethren, so that there will not be in any one of you an evil, unbelieving heart that falls away from the living God.

13 Exhort one another day by day as long as it is still called "today," so that no one will be hardened by the deceitfulness of sin.

14 For we have all become partakers of Christ if we hold fast the confidence we had in the beginning firm to the end,

15 while it is said, "Today if you will hear His voice, do not harden your hearts, as in the provocation" (see Psalm 95:7-8).

16 For who, when they heard, did the provoking? Did not all who came out of Egypt with Moses?

17 With whom was He displeased for forty years? Was it not with those who sinned, whose bodies fell in the wilderness?

18 To whom did He swear that they should not enter into His rest, but to those who were disobedient?

19 So we see that they were not able to enter in because of unbelief.

Consider Jesus

Hebrews 3:1-19: Here Moses is honored as one of the greatest servants of God of all time. Even so, Jesus is not a servant, but the Son. Jesus did not just build the model by which the atonement sacrifice could be understood, as Moses did with the tabernacle. Jesus was the Sacrifice. As we are told in chapter one of the Gospel of John, Colossians, and other Scriptures, the world was created by Jesus. Therefore, the Builder of the house deserves more honor than the house.

An important message from the model is that while the Lord was calling forth His people through Moses to leave their bondage and go to the Promised Land, those who lacked faith did not enter. We too have been called out of bondage by Jesus, the true Deliverer who Moses was a type of. Therefore, how much more faith should we have in His ability to lead us into our Promised Land?

NOTES

The Epistle to the
HEBREWS
Hebrews 4

Entering His Rest

1 Let us fear therefore, while there is still a promise of entering into His rest, that any one of you should seem to have come short of it.

2 For indeed we have had good news preached to us, even as they also did, but the word they heard did not profit them, because it was not united by faith with those who heard.

3 For we who have believed do enter into that rest, even as He has said, "As I swore in My wrath, 'They shall not enter into My rest'" (see Psalm 95:11) although the works were finished from the foundation of the world.

4 For He has said somewhere of the seventh day concerning this, "God rested on the seventh day from all His works" (see Genesis 2:2);

5 and in this place again, "They shall not enter into My rest."

6 Seeing therefore that it remains for some to enter into His rest, and they to whom the good news was preached failed to enter in because of disobedience,

7 He again defines a certain day, "Today," saying through David so long a time afterward even as has been said before, "Today if you will hear His voice, do not harden your hearts" (see Psalm 95:7).

8 If Joshua had given them rest he would not have spoken of another day afterward.

9 There remains therefore a Sabbath rest for the people of God.

10 For he that has entered into His rest has himself rested from his own works, just as God did from His.

11 Let us therefore be diligent to enter into that rest so that no man falls after the same example of disobedience.

The Power of His Word

12 For the word of God is living, and active, and sharper than any two-edged sword, piercing even to the dividing of soul and spirit, of both joints and marrow, and is quick to discern the thoughts and intents of the heart.

13 There is no creature that is not manifest in His sight, but all things are naked and laid open before the eyes of Him with whom we have to do.

14 Having then a great High Priest, who has passed through the heavens, Jesus the Son of God, let us hold fast to our confession.

15 For we do not have a High Priest who cannot be touched with the feeling of our infirmities, but one that has been in all points tempted in the same way that we have, but without sin.

16 Let us therefore be bold to draw near to the throne of grace, that we may receive mercy, and may find grace to help us in time of need.

Entering His Rest

Hebrews 4:1-11: One consequence of the Fall was the curse of toil. Work itself is not toil, but toil is defined as work accomplished with great and painful effort. Spiritual toil is seeking to base our righteousness on our own works, which can never be done. We can never measure up, and therefore, we can never rest. Here the Promised Land is equated with entering God's rest, which we do by ceasing from our own works. We enter into His finished work by believing in His propitiation for our sin and that He is our righteousness. We have turmoil when we look to ourselves. We have peace and rest when we look to Him.

Trust in God is the basis for a peace and rest that cannot be attained any other way. This begins with believing in His work on the cross as the basis of our righteousness, our salvation,

and the door through which we enter our Promised Land, the fulfillment of the promises. When we see the work that He has already accomplished, we can cease striving.

The Power of His Word

4:12-16: Immediately after the discourse on how we enter God's rest, we have a description of how the Word of God acts as a sword to divide between soul and spirit. This division works to expose things that are hidden. Many things that are hidden deep within us keep us from trusting God. Selfish ambition, lust, greed, guilt, or other such things keep us striving rather than trusting God. This exposure by the Word of God helps to set us free from such bondage. When we are fully exposed, let us not run away from God, but to Him. Let us come boldly before His throne on the basis of the blood of Jesus, not our own righteousness.

NOTES

THE EPISTLE TO THE
HEBREWS

Hebrews 5

One Mediator

1 Every high priest taken from among men is appointed for men in things pertaining to God so that he may offer both gifts and sacrifices for sins.

2 He can bear gently with the ignorant and erring, because he himself is also beset with weakness,

3 and by reason of this is obligated to make offerings for sins, for the people and also for himself.

4 No man takes this honor to himself, but only when he is called by God, even as Aaron was.

5 So Christ did not glorify Himself to be made a high priest, but He that spoke to Him said, "You are My Son, this day have I begotten You" (see Psalm 2:7).

Melchizedek

6 He said also in another place, "You are a priest forever after the order of Melchizedek" (see Psalm 110:4).

7 In the days when He walked in the flesh, having offered up prayers and supplications with strong crying, and tears to Him that was able to save Him from death, and having been heard because of His godly fear,

8 though He was a Son, yet He learned obedience by the things that He suffered.

9 Having been made perfect, He became to all who obey Him the Author of eternal salvation,

10 and was named by God a high priest after the order of Melchizedek.

11 About Him we have many things to say, and the interpretation will be hard to understand, especially since you have become dull of hearing.

12 For now, by reason of the time you have been in the faith, you should be teachers, yet you have need for someone to teach you again the fundamental principles of the oracles of God. You have become like those who need milk, and not of solid food.

13 Every one that partakes of milk is without maturity in the word of righteousness because he is a babe.

14 Solid food is for the mature, even those who by reason of use have their senses exercised to discern good and evil.

One Mediator

Hebrews 5:1-5: We see here that the priesthood was designed by God to be a compassionate mediator for the people in regard to their sin. Jesus, the ultimate High Priest, would also have the ultimate compassion because He proved His love for us by sacrificing Himself. He also, as the Mediator of "a better covenant," does not only forgive sin, but He has given His Holy Spirit to empower His people to overcome sin.

Melchizedek

5:6-14: Jesus is not a priest according to the Order of Aaron, but Melchizedek. Melchizedek was one of the most mysterious people in the Old Testament. He represents the eternal nature of Christ's priesthood, being both a king and a high priest, and therefore he was a type of the coming "royal priesthood." Many theologians believe that this was Christ who manifested Himself to Abraham. Perhaps, but we do need to understand Melchizedek if we are to understand our priesthood in the New Covenant in Christ.

One of the first things said of Melchizedek is that he was from Salem. Salem means "peace." The peace of God is one of the most basic gifts of God that we must walk in if we are going to walk in the priesthood we are called to. Jesus is the Prince of Peace, and He will rule from Jerusalem, which means "city of peace." Even though the Lord uses the title "Lord of hosts," or "Lord of armies" over ten times more than all His other titles, we are told in Romans 16:20 that it is the "God of peace" who will crush Satan under our feet. It is the peace of God that is an impregnable fortress for our souls. We are told that it is the peace of God that will guard our hearts and minds in Christ Jesus (see Philippians 4:7).

It is a basic purpose of the priesthood to sanctify the people for service to the Lord. As we are told in I Thessalonians 5:23-24, "Now may the God of peace Himself sanctify you entirely; and may your spirit and soul and body be preserved complete, without blame at the coming of our Lord Jesus Christ." Knowing the peace of God and the God of peace is fundamental to walking in our priestly calling.

Some today claim that tithing—giving the first ten percent of our income or produce to the Lord—is no longer required because that was from the law. It is true that we are no longer under the yoke of the law for our righteousness, but to think that we no longer comply with anything written in the law is to wrongly apply this truth. The command not to murder was also part of the law, but just because we are no longer under the law does not mean that we are now free to murder. There are many things that were part of the law that we are still required to do, such as loving God above all things, loving one another, not murdering or stealing, etc.

Tithing was actually pre-law. We first see it in Scripture with Abraham paying a tithe to Melchizedek. Isaac and Jacob continued this practice. This is basic to being a part of the Melchizedek priesthood. This is an honor and privilege. When we do not understand and practice this, we are missing one of the greatest blessings and a major part of our lives is denied the sanctification to which we are called. Good stewardship

is basic to biblical righteousness, and tithing is basic to good stewardship.

NOTES

THE EPISTLE TO THE
HEBREWS
Hebrews 6

The Basic Doctrines of the Faith

1 Therefore, leaving the elementary principles about the Christ, let us press on to maturity, not laying again the foundation of repentance from dead works and of faith toward God,

2 or the teaching about baptisms, the laying on of hands, the resurrection of the dead, or eternal judgment.

3 This will we do if God permits.

Falling Away

4 As to those who were once enlightened, and tasted of the heavenly gift, and were made partakers of the Holy Spirit,

5 and tasted the good word of God, and the powers of the age to come,

6 and then fell away, it is impossible to renew them again to repentance, because they crucify to themselves the Son of God again, and put Him to an open shame.

7 The land that has drunk the rain that often comes upon it, and brings forth herbs for those for who tilled it, receives a blessing from God.

8 However, if it bears thorns and thistles, it is rejected and near to being cursed, and it will ultimately be burned.

9 Beloved, we are persuaded of better things concerning you, that which accompanies salvation, though we must remind you of these things.

10 God is not unrighteous to forget your work, and the love that you showed toward His name, how you ministered to the saints, and still do minister.

Inheriting the Promises

11 We desire that each one of you may show the same diligence to keep the fullness of hope even to the end,

12 so that you may not be sluggish, but imitators of those who through faith and patience inherit the promises.

13 When God made the promise to Abraham, since He could swear by no one greater, He swore by Himself,

14 saying, "Surely with blessings I will bless you, and multiply you" (see Genesis 22:17).

15 In this way, having patiently endured, he obtained the promise.

16 For men swear by the one who is greater, and in every dispute of theirs the oath is final for confirmation.

17 In this way God, being determined to show more abundantly to the heirs of the promise the immutability of His counsel, declared with an oath

18 that by two immutable things in which it is impossible for God to lie, we may have great encouragement who have fled for refuge in Him in order to lay hold of the hope set before us.

19 This hope we have as an anchor for the soul, a hope both sure and steadfast, and that enters within the veil,

20 where Jesus, as a forerunner, entered for us, having become a High Priest forever after the order of Melchizedek.

The Basic Doctrines of Faith

The seven basic Christian doctrines are stated in Hebrews 6:1-3:

1) Christ

2) repentance

3) faith

4) baptisms

5) the laying on of hands

6) resurrection

7) eternal judgment

To the degree that we know these and walk in them, we have built our lives on a strong foundation. Those who are the most successful in any field are those who do the basics best. The most successful Christians will build their lives firmly upon these basics.

The exhortation to leave the elementary teachings about Christ to grow into maturity does not mean that we leave the teachings about Christ; we are just to leave the elementary teachings about Him to continue on to the more advanced teachings about Christ. Christ is everything, as we are told that all things will be summed up in Him (see Ephesians 1). True maturity is growing up in all things into Him (see Ephesians 4). Though we should go on beyond the elementary teachings about Christ, we never leave the teachings about Christ.

Falling Away

6:4-10: This does not mean that if one falls away they can never be renewed. However, there is a certain level of maturity and experience in God that is described here. If one has attained this and then falls away, they would already be incorrigible.

Inheriting the Promises

6:11-20: Diligence, endurance, faith, and patience are required to inherit the promises. These separate the ones who truly value the calling of God from those who are like Esau, who cared so little about it that he would sell his birthright for the temporary gratification of his appetite.

Since it takes "faith and patience" to inherit the promises, why do we have such a great "faith movement" but no "patience movement"? It takes both. Faith without patience is not really faith. One reason so many feel that what they were expecting by faith fell short is because they left out half of the ingredients.

NOTES

THE EPISTLE TO THE
HEBREWS

Hebrews 7

Tithing to Melchizedek

1 For this Melchizedek, king of Salem, priest of the Most High God, who met Abraham returning from the slaughter of the kings, and blessed him.

2 To *him* also Abraham gave a tenth of all the spoil, whose name is first, by interpretation King of Righteousness, and then also King of Salem, which is King of Peace.

3 He is without father, without mother, without genealogy, having neither beginning of days nor end of life, but made like the Son of God, a priest who abides continually.

4 Now consider how great this man was to whom Abraham, the patriarch, gave a tenth of the spoils.

5 So they indeed who are of the sons of Levi that receive the priest's office have a commandment to take tithes from the people according to the law, that is, of their brethren, though these have come out of the loins of Abraham,

6 but he whose genealogy is not counted from them has taken tithes from Abraham, and has blessed him who has the promises.

7 Without any dispute the lesser is blessed of the greater.

8 Here men that die receive tithes, but this one, it is witnessed that he lives on.

9 So we can say that through Abraham even Levi, who receives tithes, has paid tithes,

10 as he was yet in the loins of his father when Melchizedek met him.

The Melchizedek Priesthood

11 Now if there was perfection through the Levitical priesthood, for under it the people received the law, what further need was there that another priest should arise after the order of Melchizedek, and not after the order of Aaron?

12 For when the priesthood is changed there is a necessity also that there be a change of the law.

13 For He of whom these things are said belong to another tribe, from which no man has served at the altar.

14 For it is evident that our Lord came forth from Judah, as to which tribe Moses spoke nothing concerning priests.

15 What can we say? This is yet more abundantly evident, if after the likeness of Melchizedek there arises another priest,

16 who has been made a priest not after the law of carnal commandment, but after the power of an everlasting life,

17 for it is witnessed of Him, "You are a priest forever after the order of Melchizedek" (see Psalm 110:4).

18 For there is an annulling of the former commandment because of its weakness and unfruitfulness.

A Better Covenant

19 The law made nothing perfect, and now we have been given a better hope through which we draw near to God.

20 Inasmuch as it is not without the taking of an oath because they have been made priests without an oath,

21 but He with an oath by the One that says of Him, "The Lord swore, and will not repent, 'You are a priest forever'" (see Psalm 110:4),

22 by so much Jesus has also become the guarantee of a better covenant.

23 They indeed have many who were made priests, because by death they are hindered from continuing,

24 but He, because He abides forever, has His priesthood continually.

25 Therefore He is able to save to the uttermost those who draw near to God through Him, seeing that He ever lives to make intercession for them.

One Sacrifice Enough for All

26 For such a high priest became for us, holy, guileless, undefiled, separated from sinners, and made higher than the heavens,

27 who unlike those high priests, does not need to daily offer up sacrifices, first for His own sins, and then for the sins of the people, for this He did once for all when He offered up Himself.

28 For the law appoints men high priests who have weaknesses, but the word of the oath, which was after the law, appoints a Son, perfected for evermore.

Tithing to Melchizedek

Hebrews 7:1-10: In the middle of this discourse about the foundational New Covenant principles, the mysterious Melchizedek is again the focus. He is the King of Righteousness and the King of Peace, yet he appears to collect a tithe of the spoil from the slaughter of the kings by Abraham. Why would he endorse this conflict? There are righteous wars, and if we would fight them with the resolve Abraham had, we would actually have a more enduring peace.

The Melchizedek Priesthood

7:11-18: Tithing is a basic part of the New Covenant because Jesus is the High Priest after the Order of Melchizedek, who received tithes even from Abraham.

Many theologians believe that Melchizedek was actually the Lord Jesus Himself, the Son of God who is our "only mediator between God and men."

A Better Covenant

7:19-25: That we have "a better covenant" through Christ is evident. We are given the Holy Spirit to live in us, not just come upon us at times. By this there is regeneration so that we are born again and can have our minds transformed until we not only see God as He is, as perfectly demonstrated through Christ Jesus, but we begin to see as God does, having His mind and heart.

Having "a better covenant" also means that the greatest grace and power experienced under the Old Covenant should be the floor upon which we experience the New Covenant. This is why Paul wrote in II Corinthians 3 that we who are of the New Covenant should be experiencing more glory than Moses did.

One Sacrifice Enough for All

7:26-28: Jesus' sacrifice on the cross only needed to be done once. It was enough for all—for all sins and for all time. We should consider any doctrine that would detract from this an attack against the most important truth of our faith. The cross of Jesus alone is the basis of our salvation, our reconciliation, and our restoration to the Father. His cross was enough to atone for all sin for all time. This cannot be added to or detracted from.

NOTES

THE EPISTLE TO THE
HEBREWS

Hebrews 8

The New Covenant

1 Now in the things that we are saying the chief point is this: We have such a High Priest who sat down on the right hand of the throne of the Majesty in the heavens,

2 a minister of the sanctuary, and of the true tabernacle, that the Lord pitched, not man.

3 For every high priest is appointed to offer both gifts and sacrifices, therefore it is necessary that this high priest also have something to offer.

4 Now if He were on earth, He would not be a priest at all, seeing there are those who offer the gifts according to the law,

5 who serve that which is a copy and shadow of the heavenly things, even as Moses is warned by God when he is about to make the tabernacle: "'See,' says He, 'that you make all things according to the pattern that was shown to you on the mountain'" (see Exodus 25:40).

6 He has obtained a more excellent ministry because He is the Mediator of a better covenant, which has been enacted upon better promises.

7 For if that first covenant had not been lacking then there would have been no need for a second.

8 Finding its lack, He says, "'Behold, the days will come,' says the Lord, 'that I will make a new covenant with the house of Israel and with the house of Judah;

9 'not according to the covenant that I made with their fathers, in the day that I took them by the hand to lead them out of the land of Egypt. For they did not continue in My covenant, and I did not regard them,' says the Lord.

10 'For this is the covenant that I will make with the house of Israel after those days,' says the Lord; 'I will put My laws into their mind, and I will write them on their hearts, and I will be their God, and they will be My people.

11 'Then they will not teach every man his fellow-citizen, and every man his brother, saying, "'Know the Lord,'" For all will know Me, from the least to the greatest of them.

12 'For I will be merciful with their iniquities, and I will not remember their sins any longer'" (see Jeremiah 31:31-34).

13 Because He says, "A new covenant," He has made the first old, and that which is becoming old and aged is near to vanishing away.

The New Covenant

Hebrews 8:1-13: The entire Old Covenant was a prophecy pointing to the New Covenant that was established through Christ. The first covenant was a prophetic model of the coming covenant as well as an instructor laying a foundational understanding of sin and the sacrifice of the Lamb of God. Once we have partaken of the New Covenant, it is a basic departure from the grace of God to return to the old.

NOTES

THE EPISTLE TO THE
HEBREWS
Hebrews 9

The Tabernacle

1   Now even the first covenant had ordinances of divine service, and its sanctuary was on this world.

2   For there was a tabernacle prepared which is called the Holy Place, and in the first compartment there was the candlestick, and the table of showbread.

3   After the second veil there is the tabernacle called the Holy of Holies,

4   having a golden altar of incense, and the ark of the covenant, overlaid all over with gold, which held the golden pot of manna, Aaron's rod that budded, and the tablets of the covenant.

5   Above it were the cherubim of glory overshadowing the mercy seat, which we cannot now speak about.

6   Now with these things having been prepared in this way, the priests go in continually into the first tabernacle performing the divine worship.

7   Into the second the high priest went alone, once a year, and not without blood that he offered for himself and for the sins of the people.

8   The Holy Spirit is signifying this: the way into the Holy Place has not yet been made manifest while the first tabernacle is still standing.

9   It is a type, or shadow, for the present time. According to these were offered both gifts and sacrifices that cannot touch the conscience, or make the worshiper perfect,

10 since they relate to only food and drink, and different external cleansing ordinances, imposed until the time of reformation.

A Better Tabernacle for a Better Covenant

11 Christ has become a High Priest of the good things to come, through the greater and more perfect tabernacle that was not made with hands, that is to say, not of this creation.

12 It is not through the blood of goats and calves, but through His own blood that He took once and for all into the Holy Place, having obtained eternal redemption.

13 For if the blood of goats and bulls, and the ashes of a heifer sprinkling them that have been defiled, sanctify for the cleansing of the flesh,

14 how much more shall the blood of Christ, who through the eternal Spirit offered Himself without blemish to God, cleanse your conscience from dead works to serve the living God?

15 For this cause He is the Mediator of a New Covenant, with a death having taken place for the redemption of the transgressions that were under the first covenant, so they that have been called may receive the promise of the eternal inheritance.

The Power of the Blood

16 For where a covenant is made, there must of necessity be the death of him that made it.

17 For a last will and testament is enforced only when there has been death, for it is not valid while he that made it is still alive.

18 Therefore even the first covenant was not dedicated without blood.

19 When every commandment had been stated by Moses to all the people according to the law, he took the blood of the calves and the goats, with water and scarlet wool and hyssop, and sprinkled both the book itself and all the people,

20 saying, "This is the blood of the covenant that God commanded for you" (see Exodus 24:8).

21 Also, the tabernacle, and all the vessels of the ministry, he sprinkled in like manner with the blood.

22 According to the law we might say almost all things are cleansed with blood, and apart from the shedding of blood there is no remission of sins.

23 It was necessary therefore that the copies of the things in the heavens should be cleansed with these, but the heavenly things themselves with better sacrifices than these.

24 For Christ did not enter into a holy place made with hands, like the pattern, but into heaven itself, now to appear before the face of God for us.

25 Neither was it required for Him to offer Himself often, as the high priest used to enter into the holy place year by year with blood that was not his own,

26 or else He would have had to suffer often since the foundation of the world. But now, once at the end of the ages, He has been manifested to put away sin by the sacrifice of Himself.

27 Inasmuch as it is appointed to men to die once, and after this comes the judgment,

28 so Christ also, having been offered once to bear the sins of many, will appear a second time, not for sin, but for those who wait for Him, for salvation.

The Tabernacle

Hebrews 9:1-10: Everywhere in the Old Testament that the furniture of the tabernacle is mentioned, the altar of incense is in the Holy Place with the table of showbread and the lampstand, placed against the curtain that leads to the Holy of Holies. In this text, the only place it is mentioned in the New Testament, the altar of incense has moved into the Holy of Holies. As incense represents prayer and worship in Scripture, this speaks that it is through prayer and worship that we enter into the very presence of the Lord.

In verse 6, we are told that the priests were "continually" entering the Holy Place performing the divine service. This speaks of how we are to remain continually in a place of worship and intercession before the Lord.

A Better Tabernacle for a Better Covenant

9:11-15: This is one of the most important truths of the New Covenant—the blood of Jesus offered at the cross cleanses us from sin. No amount of sacrifice could ever equal the cross. To even consider that anything we could do is acceptable in place of the sacrifice of His Son is an ultimate affront to the Son and His sacrifice.

We are told that the sprinkling of the blood of animals was able to cleanse the flesh, but not the heart or conscience. The blood of Jesus will cleanse our evil consciences so that all of the remorse for all of our failures is washed away and replaced with the joy of the Lord.

The Power of the Blood

9:16-28: Here it is again explained that the tabernacle on earth was a model of the heavenly tabernacle that was given to instruct in the basic spiritual principles and the path to redemption. Jesus did not enter the model. He entered the true tabernacle of God in heaven. He presented His blood before the Father to forever make the way for those who trust in His sacrifice to come to the Father.

In verse 25, we are again assured that Christ did not have to offer Himself often for our sins, but the one sacrifice of His cross was enough for all and for all time. Any doctrine that would contradict this is a false doctrine that undermines the very power of the New Covenant that was consummated for us by the cross of Jesus alone. His sacrifice, having been made once, was enough.

Historical Note:

The doctrine which claimed that Christ needed to be offered repeatedly for our daily sins is called "the sacrifice of the mass" or "transubstantiation." It was a main point of conflict which arose in The Reformation. Many Reformers considered this "the abomination of desolation," or as this could have been literally translated, "the abomination that desolates," spoken of by the Prophet Daniel. They believed that this doctrine supplanted the power of the cross of Jesus in the Christian's daily and personal life, placing a man, another priest, in the place of Christ as our mediator. This sacrifice of the mass, which had to be done repeatedly, is a violation of Hebrews 7:26-28 that states clearly that Jesus made the acceptable sacrifice which was enough for all and for all time.

The "Early Church Fathers," who were the disciples of the original twelve apostles, all taught that the antichrist would take his seat in the temple of God which is the church. There is no mention in their writings of a rebuilding of the physical temple. They saw the antichrist as not just one who opposed Christ, but one who sought to become a substitute for Christ. Many Reformers believed this doctrine of the mass essentially supplanted Christ in the life of believers. For this reason, most Reformation churches taught that the Roman Papacy was the antichrist that had been prophesied by the apostles.

Even so, some prominent Reformers, such as Martin Luther, though believing the Papacy to be the antichrist, still held to this doctrine of transubstantiation and continued to use it in their churches. It is generally accepted that about fifty million Protestants were martyred by the Roman church during the Inquisition and other attacks. Because Rome was called "The City of Seven Hills," and "Mystery Babylon," spoken of in the Book of Revelation, sat on a "city of seven hills," it was accepted doctrine in virtually all Protestant churches and movements that the Papacy was the antichrist. This was universal until the 1844 Advent Movement formulated the eschatology that placed almost everything prophesied in the Books of Daniel and Revelation to the future.

Regardless of whether one holds to this doctrine or not, the Protestant churches ended up persecuting Anabaptists and other future movements, using most of the diabolical methods employed by some Catholic zealots during the Inquisition and other persecutions of Protestants. Many of the movements persecuted by the Protestants in turn persecuted others who would not comply with their doctrine. We need to know and understand these historical events so that we do not keep repeating them.

Even more so, we need to put our full trust in the sacrifice of Jesus on His cross and not let any other teaching of man dilute or substitute the cross of Jesus as our salvation.

NOTES

THE EPISTLE TO THE
HEBREWS
Hebrews 10

A Better Sacrifice

1 For the law, being a shadow of the good things to come, not the very substance of them, can never make perfect those who draw near, even with the same sacrifices year by year that they offer continually.

2 If they had, would they not have ceased to be offered? Yes, because the worshipers, having once been cleansed, would have had no more consciousness of sins.

3 However, in those sacrifices there is a remembrance made of the sins year by year,

4 because it is impossible that the blood of bulls and goats could take away sin.

5 Therefore, when He comes into the world, He says, "Sacrifice and offering you would not receive, but a body You did prepare for Me.

6 "In whole burnt offerings, and sacrifices for sin, You had no pleasure.

7 "Then I said, 'Behold, I have come, as in the scroll of the book it is written of Me, to do Your will, O God'" (see Psalm 40:6-8).

8 As the above states, sacrifices and offerings, and even whole burnt offerings and sacrifices for sin, He would not receive, neither did He have pleasure in these things that are offered according to the law.

9 Then He says, "Behold, I have come to do Your will" (see Psalm 40:8). He takes away the first so that He may establish the second.

10 By this we have been sanctified through the offering of the body of Jesus Christ once for all.

11 Every priest indeed stands day by day ministering, and offering many times the same sacrifices that can never take away sins,

12 but He, when He had offered one sacrifice for sins forever, sat down at the right hand of God,

13 from this time waiting until His enemies are made a footstool for His feet.

14 For by one offering He has perfected forever those who are sanctified.

15 The Holy Spirit also bears witness to us, for after this He has said,

16 "'This is the covenant that I will make with them after those days,' says the Lord: 'I will put My laws on their heart, and upon their mind I will write them,'" then He says,

17 "and their sins and their iniquities I will remember no more" (see Jeremiah 31:33-34).

18 Now where there is a remission of these, there is no need for an offering for sin.

19 Having therefore, brethren, boldness to enter into the holy place by the blood of Jesus,

20 by the way that He dedicated for us, a new and living way, through the veil, that is to say, His body.

21 Having such a great priest over the house of God,

22 let us draw near with a true heart in the fullness of faith, having our hearts sprinkled clean from an evil conscience, and having our body washed with pure water,

23 let us hold fast the confession of our hope without wavering, for He is faithful that promised.

Devoted to Fellowship

24 Let us therefore consider how to provoke one another to love and good works,

25 not forsaking our own assembling together, as is the custom of some, but exhorting one another, and so much the more as you see the day drawing near.

Penalty of Willful Sin

26 If we sin willfully after we have received the knowledge of the truth, there no longer remains a sacrifice for sins,

27 but a certain fearful expectation of judgment, and a fury of fire that will devour the adversaries.

28 If a man that has disregarded the Law of Moses will die without compassion on the word of two or three witnesses,

29 of how much worse punishment do you think he shall be judged worthy of who has trodden under foot the Son of God, and has counted the blood of the covenant by which he was sanctified as an unholy thing, and has done this despite the Spirit of grace?

30 For we know Him that said, "Vengeance belongs to Me. I will have recompense" (see Deuteronomy 32:35). And again, "The Lord will judge His people" (see Deuteronomy 32:36).

31 It is a fearful thing to fall into the hands of the living God.

The Reward of Obedience

32 Instead, call to remembrance the former days, in which, after you were enlightened you endured great conflict, and suffered,

33 partly by being made a laughingstock, both by reproaches and afflictions, and partly by becoming partakers with those who were so treated.

34 For you both had compassion on those who were in bonds, and took it joyfully when your possessions were seized, knowing that you have for yourselves a better possession, and an abiding one.

35 Therefore, do not cast away your boldness that has a great recompense and reward.

36 For you have need of endurance, so that, having done the will of God, you may receive what was promised.

37 "For yet in a little while, He that is coming will come, and will not delay (see Habakkuk 2:3).

38 As He said, "My righteous one shall live by faith, and if he shrinks back, My soul will have no pleasure in him" (see Habakkuk 2:4).

39 We are not of those who shrink back into perdition, but of those who have faith to the saving of the soul.

A Better Sacrifice

Hebrews 10:1-23: The author continues to exhort us to know the power and excellence of the sacrifice of Jesus. Once we behold the cross—its genius, its nobility, its unequaled and unprecedented expression of love—we are given boldness to be able to approach the Father. This we can never do through our own righteousness, but only through the excellence of the sacrifice of the Son.

Verses 10-12 present us with a third reminder that Jesus did not have to offer Himself often, but once for our sins. His one sacrifice is enough and will always be enough for our redemption and reconciliation.

In verse 22, we are told that our hearts are sprinkled clean from an "evil conscience." The older you get, the more regrets you will likely have. This guilt for our previous shortcomings can be an increasing weight, keeping us from doing what we should do in the present. Jesus suffered on the cross to deliver us from this remorse. The way His blood is applied to our lives so that we are cleansed from this is also given to us here—we must draw near to God with a resolute heart, full of faith in what He did, not remorse in what we did not do, and hold fast to this confession without wavering.

Devoted to Fellowship

10:24-25: One of the most basic results of having received redemption and reconciliation is being drawn to the fellowship of the redeemed and becoming members of His body, functioning together. However, this exhortation not to forsake the

assembling is not about church services, but rather how we are to be "assembled together" in the body of Christ. This is like putting together the parts of something such as a bicycle in order to make a whole. Having all of the parts to a bicycle will not give you something to ride. The parts have to be properly fit together. When the body of Christ is merely made up of loosely associated members that have not been assembled together, we accomplish very little.

As we see in Scriptures such as I Corinthians 11 and I John 1:7, redemption and cleansing by the blood always results in unity with the body. The Greek word translated "fellowship" or "communion" in these verses is *koinonia* which is more than just a fellowship. It is such a deep intertwined bonding that we cannot live without each other.

Penalty of Willful Sin

10:26-31: This addresses a major controversy in the church that remains to this day. The sacrifice of Jesus was made to deliver us from sin. This is not so that we can go on living in sin and be forgiven. It is to deliver us from the sin itself. This is done first by our forgiveness and the relief from guilt, but then we are empowered by His Holy Spirit to live holy before Him.

Those who presume they can continue in sin because they will be forgiven are living under a presumption that is a basic affront to the cross, and they deserve the worst judgment. However, the Lord is often patient and slow to bring judgment. One of the great examples of how He gives those in even the worst error time to repent is in Revelation where He even gave Jezebel "time to repent" (see Revelation 2:20-21). Even so, we should never take this patience as the overlooking of our sin.

The Reward of Obedience

10:32-39: This age is for the purpose of allowing the testing of the righteous. Therefore, we should endure it with the true joy of knowing that it is working eternal qualities in us that will

benefit us and His coming kingdom. Those who shrink back because of persecution reveal they love this present world more than Him, but those with true faith will not shrink back.

NOTES

THE EPISTLE TO THE
HEBREWS

Hebrews 11

The Nature of Faith

1 Now faith is the assurance of things hoped for, the conviction of things not seen.

2 It was by their faith that the ancient ones gained approval.

3 By faith we understand that the worlds were formed by the word of God, and what is seen was not made out of things that appear.

The Exploits of Faith

4 By faith Abel offered to God a more excellent sacrifice than Cain, through which he received the testimony that he was righteous. God bears witness in regard to his gifts, and though he is dead he still speaks.

5 By faith Enoch was translated so that he did not see death. He was not found, because God translated him, as He had the witness concerning him before his translation that he was well-pleasing to God.

6 Without faith it is impossible to please Him, for he who comes to God must believe that He is, and that He will reward those who seek Him.

7 By faith Noah, being warned by God concerning things that had not yet been seen, moved with a godly fear, and prepared an ark for the salvation of his house. By this he judged the world, and became heir of the righteousness that is according to faith.

8   By faith Abraham, when he was called, obeyed by going out to a place that he was to receive for an inheritance. So he went out, not knowing where he was going.

9   By faith he became a sojourner in the land of promise, a land that was foreign to him, dwelling in tents with Isaac and Jacob, the heirs with him of the same promise,

10 because he was looking for the city that has foundations whose architect and builder is God.

11 By faith even Sarah herself received power to conceive a child when she was past the age, since she counted Him faithful who had promised.

12 Because of this there came forth from one, and him as good as dead in his body, a multitude like the stars of heaven, or the sand that is by the seashore that cannot be counted.

13 These all died in faith, even though they had not yet received the promises, but having seen them and welcomed them from afar, and having confessed that they were strangers and sojourners on the earth.

14 For they that say such things make it clear that they are seeking after another country of their own.

15 If they had been content with that country from which they went out, they would have had an opportunity to return.

16 But they desired a better country, that is, a heavenly one. Therefore God is not ashamed to be called their God, because He has prepared a city for them.

17 By faith Abraham, when tested, offered up Isaac. The one who had gladly received the promises was offering up his only begotten son;

18 even the one about whom it was said, "Through Isaac your seed shall be called" (see Genesis 21:12).

19 He believed that God was able to raise him up, even from the dead. For this reason he received him back as a type of Christ.

20 By faith Isaac blessed Jacob, and Esau, even concerning things to come.

21 By faith Jacob, when he was dying, blessed each of the sons of Joseph, and worshiped, leaning upon the top of his staff.

22 By faith Joseph, when his end was near, made mention of the departure of the children of Israel, and gave orders concerning his bones.

23 By faith Moses, when he was born was hidden for three months by his parents, because they saw that he was a unique child, and they were not afraid of the king's edict.

24 By faith Moses, when he had grown up, refused to be called the son of Pharaoh's daughter.

25 He chose rather to suffer affliction with the people of God than to enjoy the pleasures of sin for a season.

26 He counted the reproach of Christ as greater riches than the treasures of Egypt, because he was looking to the reward.

27 By faith he forsook Egypt, not fearing the wrath of the king, and he endured by seeing Him who is unseen.

28 By faith he kept the Passover, and the sprinkling of the blood, so that the destroyer of the firstborn could not touch them.

29 By faith they passed through the Red Sea as if they were on dry land, which the Egyptians tried to do and were swallowed up.

30 By faith the walls of Jericho fell down after they had been compassed for seven days.

31 By faith Rahab the harlot did not perish with the rest who were disobedient, having received the spies in peace.

32 What more shall I recount? For I do not have time to tell of Gideon, Barak, Samson, Jephthah, David, Samuel, and the prophets,

33 who through faith subdued kingdoms, wrought deeds of righteousness, obtained promises, stopped the mouths of lions,

34 quenched the power of fire, escaped the edge of the sword, and in weakness were made strong, becoming mighty in war, causing foreign armies to flee.

35 Women received their dead back by resurrection. Others were tortured, not accepting their deliverance so that they might obtain a better resurrection.

36 Others suffered the trials of being made a mockery, beatings, and even bonds and imprisonment.

37 They were stoned; they were sawn in two; they were tempted; they were slain by the sword. They went about in sheepskins, in goatskins, destitute, afflicted, and were ill-treated.

38 They were the ones of whom the world was not worthy, wandering in deserts, mountains, living in caves and holes in the ground.

39 All of these had the witness through their faith, but did not yet receive the promise,

40 because God, having provided something even better for us, established that apart from us they should not be completed.

The Nature of Faith

Hebrews 11:1-3: This begins the crucial explanation of what surpasses the law as our righteousness—faith. Faith calls one beyond things that are seen into the spiritual realm of God. By seeing into this realm, we receive the power to live before Him and the ability to do His works. True faith is simply seeing the Lord and where He sits above all rule and authority and dominion.

The Exploits of Faith

11:4-40: The testimony of those who devoted their earthly life for a heavenly calling, whether in the way they lived or died, is a testimony of the power of faith in God. Almost all were just ordinary men and women who simply had extraordinary faith. Faith is the law of gravity for the kingdom, and the laws of the kingdom trump any earthly, natural law. Through the laws of the heavenly kingdom, which is the power of the King, we do exploits on the earth.

The one common denominator shared by all these heroes of the faith is that they did something no one had ever done before. They were creative in their faith, and such creativity is what carries us beyond ordinary human limits. It takes an

exceptional faith to do what has not been done before. It is this faith that touches the heart of the Creator in a special way. True faith does not resort to patterns and formulas, which is a root of witchcraft, rather true faith is creative.

Verse 27 may be the one statement that best explains such great faith. It says that Moses "endured as seeing Him who is unseen." What Moses and all of these others saw with their spiritual eyes was more real to them than what they saw with their natural eyes. They lived by a greater reality. Do we?

NOTES

THE EPISTLE TO THE
HEBREWS
Hebrews 12

Call to Endurance

1   Seeing that we are surrounded by such a great cloud of witnesses, let us lay aside every encumbrance and the sin that so easily entangles us, and let us run with endurance the race that is set before us.

2   Look to Jesus, the author and finisher of our faith, who for the joy set before Him endured the cross, despising shame, and has sat down at the right hand of the throne of God.

3   For consider Him who has endured such opposition from sinners against Himself so that you may not grow weary and lose heart.

4   You have not yet resisted to the point of shedding blood in your striving against sin,

5   and you have forgotten the exhortation that appeals to you as with sons, "My son, do not regard lightly the chastening of the Lord, or faint when you are reproved by Him.

6   "For it is the ones whom the Lord loves that He chastens, and He scourges every son whom He receives" (see Proverbs 3:11-12).

Call to Discipline

7   It is for discipline that you endure. God deals with you as with sons. What son is there whom his father does not discipline?

8   If you are without discipline, of which all have been made partakers, then you are illegitimate children, and not sons.

9 We had our fathers according to the flesh who chastened us, and we revered them. Should we not even more subject ourselves to the Father of spirits and live?

10 For they chastened us for a short time, for our good in the way that they thought was right, but He knows what will truly profit us so that we may be partakers of His holiness.

11 All chastening is hard, and it is hard to be joyful when enduring it, but we are understandably grieved, yet afterward it yields the peaceful fruit of righteousness for those who have endured it.

12 Therefore, lift up the hands that are limp, strengthen your weak knees,

13 and make straight paths for your feet so that limb that is lame will not be cut off, but rather be healed.

Peace and Sanctification

14 Seek peace with all men, and the sanctification without which no one will see the Lord.

15 Always be on the watch for anyone who falls short of the grace of God, and for any root of bitterness that springs up to trouble you, and by it many be defiled.

16 Be on guard against any form of fornication, or for a profane person like Esau, who for a single meal sold his own birthright.

17 For you know that when he later desired to inherit the blessing he was rejected, as it was too late for him to change his mind though he sought for it diligently with tears.

An Awesome God

18 For you have not come to a mountain that might be touched, and that burns with fire, to the gloom of a storm, or the darkness of a tempest,

19 to the sound of a trumpet, and the voice speaking words with such power that those who heard them begged that no more words should be spoken to them.

20 They could not endure the command that "if even a beast touched the mountain, it shall be stoned" (see Exodus 19:12).

21 So fearful was the scene that even Moses said, "I am trembling with fear!" (see Deuteronomy 9:19)

22 However, you have come to Mount Zion, and to the city of the living God, the heavenly Jerusalem, to the innumerable hosts of angels,

23 to the general assembly and church of the firstborn who are enrolled in heaven. You have come to God, the Judge of all, and to the spirits of just men made perfect,

24 and to Jesus, the Mediator of a new covenant, and to the blood that was sprinkled that speaks much louder than Abel's.

25 See that you do not refuse Him that is now speaking. For if they did not escape who refused him that warned them on earth, how much more shall we not escape who turn away from Him that warns from heaven,

26 whose voice shook the earth then, but now He has promised, saying, "Yet once more I will not only shake the earth, but also the heavens" (see Haggai 2:6).

27 This word, **"Yet once more,"** signifies the removing of those things that were made, and that can be shaken, so that only those things that cannot be shaken will remain.

28 Therefore, since we have received a kingdom that cannot be shaken, let us walk in this grace, and offer service that is well pleasing to God with reverence and awe,

29 for our God is a consuming fire.

Call to Endurance

Hebrews 12:1-6: The testimony of the great seekers of God can help keep us on course. They are also a loving testimony of how the Lord uses trials and discipline for those He loves. No trial comes upon us that does not have purpose. The great purpose is to teach us to walk in faith, confidence, and victory in a world that is opposed to Him and that will oppose those

who seek to walk in His ways. This opposition is allowed by Him in this age as "training for reigning" for those who have the highest calling in all of creation—His sons and daughters.

Call to Discipline

12:7-13: Every trial in our lives has a purpose that James declared was more precious than silver or gold. It is more valuable than anything on earth or that we could ever attain in this life. It is to conform us to the image of the Son, and that will last for eternity.

Peace and Sanctification

12:14-17: Even with the opposition of this world, we are to do all we can to seek peace with those who oppose us. We stand firmly against the opposition, even for the sake of those who are opposing us, so that our testimony might open their eyes to the One who went to the cross to free them from their bondage. This compels those who walk with God toward a sanctification that we must have to see and follow Him.

The great trap is to become bitter at what seems unjust and is unjust. Even so, it is the greatest opportunity we will have to be identified with Christ in His sufferings, so that we might also be joined with Him in the power of His resurrection. No one will ever be more unjustly treated than Jesus when He walked the earth. Yet we cannot be resurrected unless we have first died. The opposition of this world helps us to die daily so that we might also experience His resurrection power daily. This is why the apostles went out rejoicing after being beaten. They understood, like Moses did, that being able to share in the reproach of Christ is greater riches than all the treasures of this world.

In all that we endure for serving Him, let us never forget that all discipline is from a loving Father who is using all things to prepare us for our great calling to be heirs with His Son.

An Awesome God

12:18-29: Our great God deserves nothing less than our greatest trust and faith. In fact, no one can measure up to what He truly deserves. Yet He rewards us beyond measure for even our feeble attempts to believe Him and do His will. So let us never forget how awesome He is and remain humble even in our greatest accomplishments and attempts to serve Him. Let us boast in the Lord, not in what we have done.

NOTES

THE EPISTLE TO THE
HEBREWS

Hebrews 13

Call to Love and Righteousness

1 Let love of the brethren continue.

2 Do not neglect showing hospitality to strangers, because in doing this some have entertained angels without knowing it.

3 Remember those who are in bonds as if you are in prison with them. Remember those who are oppressed as those who are also in the body.

4 Let marriage be held in honor among all, and do not allow the marriage bed to be defiled, because God will judge fornicators and adulterers.

5 Be free from the love of money, and content with the things that you have, for He Himself has promised, saying, "I will in no way fail you, or forsake you" (see Joshua 1:5).

6 It is this that gives us such great courage so that we say, "The Lord is my Helper, I will not fear. Why should I fear what man might do to me?" (see Psalm 118:6).

7 Remember those who have authority over you, who speak the word of God to you, considering their manner of life, and imitating their faith.

8 Jesus Christ is the same yesterday, today, and forever.

9 Do not be carried away by different and strange teachings. It is good that your heart is established by grace, not by meat that could be compared to that which is forbidden by the law, and by which those who partake of it are not profited.

Going Outside the Camp

10 We have an altar from which those who serve the tabernacle cannot eat.

11 For the bodies of the animals whose blood is brought into the Holy Place by the high priest as an offering for sin are burned outside the camp.

12 Therefore Jesus also, that He might sanctify the people through His own blood, suffered outside the gate.

13 Let us therefore go to Him outside the camp, bearing His reproach.

14 For we do not here have an abiding city, but we seek the city which is to come.

15 Through Him then let us offer up a sacrifice of praise to God continually, that is, the fruit of our lips which proclaim His name.

16 Do not neglect to do good deeds, for such are the sacrifices that God is well pleased with.

Final Exhortation

17 Obey those who have authority over you, and submit to them, because they watch over your souls as those who will give account. So let them do this with joy, and not with grief, as that would not be profitable for you.

18 Pray for us, as we have faith, and a good conscience, and desire to live honorably in all things.

19 I exhort you even more to do this, so that I may be restored to you even sooner.

20 Now the God of peace who raised the great Shepherd of the sheep from the dead, through the blood of an eternal covenant, even our Lord Jesus,

21 make you complete in every way to do His will, working with us that which is well-pleasing in His sight, through Jesus Christ, to whom be the glory forever and ever. Amen.

22 But I exhort you, brethren, to bear with this word of exhortation, which I have written to you with but a few words.

23 Know that our brother Timothy has been set free, and with whom, if he comes shortly, I will bring when I see you.

24 Salute those who have authority over you, and all the saints. Those who are in Italy greet you.

25 Grace be with you all. Amen.

Call to Love and Righteousness

Hebrews 13:1-9: The last exhortation to one of the most in-depth studies of the New Covenant is to focus on the basics—love and righteousness, doing what is right in the sight of the Lord. Those who are the most successful in any field, and those who are the greatest Christians, are those who do the basics best. This does not mean that we do not go on to higher understanding, but we must, at the same time, be constantly reviewing and practicing the basics.

Going Outside the Camp

13:10-16: The early Christians were driven outside the camp of Israel, and almost every move of God since has been excluded from the camp in which it was born. Just as the early Jewish believers maintained their love for Israel, the nation and people from which they came, the right way to deal with being drivien outside the camp is to maintain our love and respect for the works of God that gave birth to us, regardless of how they might reject us. This is the keeping of the command to "honor your fathers and mothers," which has the promise of life going well for us and longevity.

Therefore, the length and fruitfulness of the new move will be determined by how those in it honor those who went before them and gave spiritual birth to them. Rejection by our spiritual fathers and mothers is, no doubt, one of the hardest things to endure, but this may be the ultimate test to see if we are worthy of the new thing God is doing. Can we walk in the most basic element of the faith and love—forgiveness? Instead of reacting and poisoning others with examples of how wrong

and bad those who rejected us are, can we return good for evil and choose to honor them like David did Saul?

Abraham went "outside the camp" when he left his home and family to seek the city that God is building. This vision kept him through all that he was to endure and through the times when he did not know where he was going. It is this same vision that has kept the true sojourners who have walked the earth since—they are looking for what God is building, not just men.

Final Exhortation

13:17-25: There is some dispute about who the author of this Epistle is, but this one closes in a way that is typical of Paul in his letters. It is also common to his letters that they end with an exhortation to hold fast to the basic disciplines of the faith such as loving the brethren, building on sound doctrine, obeying the leaders, etc. The final exhortation is for us to become complete in Christ through our relationships with one another. If it was not Paul who wrote this Epistle, then it was likely one of his closest disciples, because this theme also resonates in all of his letters.

As stated, this Epistle is regarded as the deepest theologically in the New Testament, as the Book of Romans is considered the most comprehensive. Yet the author regarded such deep revelation as milk and not yet the meat that he would like to have given his readers. Of course, there is much more that could have been spoken of concerning the symbolism in the tabernacle and the priesthoods of Aaron and Melchizedek, and many have mined them over the centuries. To know these is necessary to fully and deeply comprehend the plan of God for this age and the one to come. Even so, to have all of that knowledge without a strong grounding in the basics will only make one vulnerable to the most deadly sin—pride. Our highest calling is to love God above all things and then to love one another. The one who loves is higher than one who has knowledge. Let us seek both, but keep them in proper order.

Can we go on to the knowledge of the powers of the age to come and not become arrogant, but continue in the humility that God gives His grace to? Learning about the powers to come is not the end of the matter, but rather walking in them. That requires God's grace.

NOTES

The Epistle to The Hebrews
Proper Names and Definitions

Aaron: a teacher, lofty, mountain of strength, fluent, light bearer

Abel: vanity, breath, vapor, a city, mourning, a meadow

Abraham: father of a great multitude, exalted father

Barak: thunder, or in vain

Cain: maker; fabricator, literally smith, possession, or possessed

Cherubim: as if contending, masculine of Cherub, order of angelic being

Christ: anointed

David: well-beloved, dear

Deuteronomy: repetition of the law

Egypt: the two lands, double straights, that troubles or oppresses, anguish

Egyptians: natives of Egypt, meaning the two lands

Enoch: dedicated, disciplined, initiated, teacher

Esau: hairy, rough, he that acts or finishes

Exodus: going out, departure

Genesis: beginning

Gideon: he that bruises or breaks, a destroyer

Isaac: laughter, he shall laugh, mockery

Isaiah: the salvation of the Lord

Israel: who prevails with God, he shall be prince of God

Italy: abounding with calves or heifers

Jacob: that supplants, undermines, heel-catcher

Jephthah: God will set free

Jeremiah: exaltation of the Lord

Jericho: his moon, his month, his sweet smell

Jerusalem: vision of peace, foundation of peace, restoring or teaching of peace

Jesus: savior, deliverer, Yahweh is salvation

Joseph: increase, addition, may God add

Joshua: a savior, a deliverer

Judah: the praise of the Lord, confession

Levi: associated with him, joined

Melchizedek: king of justice, king of righteousness

Moses: taken out, drawn forth

Noah: repose, consolation, that quavers or totters

Passover: to pass or to spring over, to spare

Pharaoh: that disperses, that spoils, great house, his nakedness

Rahab: large, proud, quarrelsome, storm, act stormily, boisterous, arrogant, sea monster, strength, broad/breadth

Salem: complete or perfect peace

Samson: his sun, his service, there the second time

Samuel: heard of God, asked of God

Sarah: lady, princess, princess of the multitude, have dominion

Sin: bush, thorn

Zion: monument, raised up, sepulcher, fortification, permanent capital, barren, dry, desert

INTRODUCTION
THE EPISTLE OF JAMES

The author of this letter is generally accepted to be James, the son of Joseph and Mary, the half brother of the Lord Jesus. The style and scope of authority of this letter indicate that its author was one of exceptional standing and influence in the church. The half brother of the Lord is the only James during the time this letter was written that was of stature within the church. He had risen to the position of leader of the church in Jerusalem. The other notable James in the New Testament, who was one of the twelve and the brother of John, had been martyred by Herod. This took place at the beginning of the dispersion mentioned in this letter indicating that the letter was written after A.D. 44.

The style of the letter is pastoral. It addresses practical aspects of basic Christian living such as dealing with temptation, faith and works, and discerning the wisdom from above from that which comes from below. The sound teaching given on these topics can have a most basic impact on the life of any who follows them. They have, no doubt, helped multitudes throughout the church age live a victorious Christian life.

James seals his strong and wise counsel to believers with the motivation that the kingdom of God is coming, being preceded by the judgment of God and the coming presence of the Lord (Greek – parousia). Biblical prophecies about the end of the age indicate that these will be the three great messages at the end of this age that help prepare the church for the coming kingdom.

THE EPISTLE OF
JAMES

James 1

Overcoming Trials

1 James, a servant of God and of the Lord Jesus Christ, to the twelve tribes that are of the dispersion, greetings.

2 Count it all joy, my brethren, when you encounter various trials, knowing that the testing of your faith produces patience.

3 Let patience have its perfect work so that you may be perfect and complete, and lack nothing.

4 If any of you lack wisdom, let him ask of it from God, who gives to all liberally, and without reproach, and it will be given to him.

5 Let him ask in faith, without doubting, because he that doubts is like the waves of the sea that are driven by the wind and tossed about.

6 Let not that man think that he will receive anything from the Lord, being a double-minded man, unstable in all of his ways.

Contentment

7 Let the brother of a low position in this world glory in his high calling.

8 Let the rich consider that they have been made lower, because riches can pass away as easily as the flower of the grass.

9 For just as the sun arises with a scorching wind, and withers the grass, and causes the flowers to wilt, and the grace of their beauty quickly perishes, in the same way the riches of man can fade away in his pursuits.

Enduring Temptation

10 Blessed is the man that endures when tempted, because when he has been approved he will receive the crown of life that the Lord promised to those who love Him.

11 Let no man say when he is tempted, "I am tempted by God," because God cannot be tempted with evil, and He Himself does not tempt any man.

12 When a man is tempted it is because he is drawn away and enticed by his own lust.

13 When the lust has been conceived it brings forth sin, and sin, when it has matured, brings forth death.

14 Do not be deceived, my beloved brethren, every good gift, and every perfect gift, is from above, coming down from the Father of lights, with whom there can be no changing nor varying shadow.

15 By His own will He brought us forth by the word of truth, that we should be a kind of first fruits of all His creatures.

The Patience of Wisdom

16 You know this, my beloved brethren. However, let every man be quick to listen, but slow to speak, and slow to anger.

17 The wrath of man does not work out the righteousness of God.

18 Therefore, putting away all uncleanness, and the abundance that comes from wickedness, receive the implanted word with meekness that is able to preserve your souls.

True Religion

19 Be doers of the word, and not hearers only, who delude themselves.

20 For if anyone is a hearer of the word and not a doer, he is like a

man who beholds his natural face in a mirror, but then goes away and immediately forgets what he looks like.

21 He that looks into the perfect law, the law of liberty, and continues to walk in it, not being one who hears and then forgets, but a doer, this man will be blessed in all that he does.

22 If any man thinks of himself as religious, but does not control his tongue, he deceives himself, and his religion is in vain.

23 Pure religion that is undefiled before our God and Father is this: to visit the orphans and widows in their affliction, and to keep oneself unsoiled from the world.

Overcoming Trials

James 1:1-6: Learning to face trials with the right spirit in order to gain the most from them is a basic requirement for Christian maturity. As Paul states in Acts 14:22, it is through tribulations that we enter the kingdom of God. In every trial there is a door to the kingdom. When we understand this, trials really do become a joy.

The Greek word that is translated "double-minded" here is *dipsuchos* (dip'-soo-khos) that literally means "two-spirited," or "two souled." It is the root word from which we derive our English word "schizophrenia," which is to have multiple personalities. When we think of schizophrenia, we often think of the extreme psychological cases (which are usually demonic), but we are double-minded or even multiple-minded if we are one personality at home, another at work, another with our friends, etc. These may be superficial changes and seem harmless, but one of the basic characteristics of God is that in Him there is "no shadow of turning" (see James 1:17). He remains consistent all of the time and so will those who are becoming like Him. The different facades we take on are veils that must be removed so we can see the Lord "with an unveiled face" (see II Corinthians 3:18) and be changed by His glory.

Contentment

1:7-9: We must learn to be content with our place in life so that we can grow in the more important disciplines, character, and fruit of the Spirit, which is basic to Christian maturity.

Enduring Temptation

1:10-15: When we are strong in the basic disciplines of the faith, we will be prepared to face the temptations of our own flesh which try to seduce us, and they will not have dominion over us.

The Patience of Wisdom

1:16-18: True wisdom is always patient. It will reject the riches that come from wickedness and be content with much less that comes with integrity.

True Religion

1:19-23: Being obedient to the Word, controlling our tongues, and visiting the afflicted could sum up the definition of a righteous person who is following true religion.

NOTES

THE EPISTLE OF
JAMES

James 2

Treat All Equally

1 My brethren, do not hold your faith in our Lord Jesus Christ, the Lord of glory, together with the fear or man.

2 For if a man comes into your synagogue with a gold ring, in fine clothing, and there also comes a poor man in filthy clothing,

3 and you have a higher regard for the one who wears the fine clothing, and say, "Sit here in a good place," and you say to the poor man, "Stand back there," or "Sit under my footstool,"

4 with this do you not make a distinction among yourselves, and become judges with evil motives?

5 Listen, my beloved brethren, did God not choose the poor of this world to be rich in faith, and heirs of the kingdom that He promised to those who love Him?

6 In this way you dishonor the poor man. Is it not the rich that oppress you, and who drag you before the judgment seats?

7 Do they not blaspheme the honorable name by which you are called?

8 However, if you fulfill the royal law, according to the Scripture, "You shall love your neighbor as yourself" (see Leviticus 19:18), you do well.

9 If you live by the fear of man you will sin, and be convicted by the law as transgressors.

10 For whoever will keep the whole law, and yet stumble in one point is guilty of all.

11 For He that said, "Do not commit adultery" (see Exodus 20:13), also said, "Do not kill" (see Deuteronomy 5:17). If you do not commit adultery, but kill, you have still become a transgressor of the law.

12 So speak and act as men that are to be judged by a law of liberty.

13 For judgment will be without mercy to him that has not shown mercy, but mercy triumphs over judgment.

Faith and Works

14 What does it profit, my brethren, if a man says that he has faith, but does not have works? Can such faith save him?

15 If a brother or sister is without clothing, or lacking food,

16 and one of you says to them, "Go in peace, be warmed and filled," but does not give them the things that they need, what good does that do?

17 Even so, faith, if it does not have works, is dead by itself.

18 Yes, if a man says, "You have faith, and I have works," I say, "If you show me faith without works, I will show you my faith by my works."

19 You think that because you believe in God that you do well, but the demons also believe and tremble.

20 Will you understand, O vain man, that faith without works is useless?

21 Was not Abraham our father justified by works when he offered up Isaac his son on the altar?

22 You see that faith brought forth his works, and by works his faith was completed.

23 So the Scripture was fulfilled which said, "And Abraham believed God, and it was reckoned to him for righteousness," and he was called the friend of God.

24 You see in this way it is by works also that a man is justified, and not by faith alone.

25 In like manner was not also Rahab the harlot justified by works, in that she received the messengers, and sent them out another way?

26 For just as the body without the spirit is dead, even so faith without works is dead.

Treat All Equally

James 2:1-13: Proverbs 29:25 says "the fear of man brings a snare." In Galatians 1:10, the Apostle Paul said, "If I am still trying to please men I would not be a bond-servant of Christ." We must choose whether we will live by the fear of man or the fear of God, but we cannot live by both or we will become double-minded, which James goes on to address.

Faith and Works

2:14-26: The Reformation through Luther brought back to the church the emphasis on personal faith in God. This text from James 2 then became one of the important and emphasized texts by later movements that contended it was not enough to merely believe something, but true faith will always result in works that bring forth fruit in keeping with faith. "Faith without works is dead" because it is not true faith if no action is attached to it.

The faith that results in righteousness is not just the belief that God exists, as verse 19 explains, but it is faith in Him. The Greek word that is translated "in" throughout the New Testament in relation to believing in the Lord is the word *eis* that literally means "into." This implies not just believing that He exists, but believing into Him, or becoming one with Him.

NOTES

THE EPISTLE OF
JAMES

James 3

The Power of Words

1 My brethren, do not let many of you become teachers, knowing that we will receive a stricter judgment.

2 We all stumble in many ways, but if anyone does not stumble in what he says he is a perfect man, able to control the whole body also.

3 We put the horses' bridles in their mouths so that they will obey us, and we can turn their whole body with it.

4 In the same way ships, though they are large, and are driven by strong winds, yet they are turned by a very small rudder in the direction of the pilot's will.

5 Likewise, the tongue is also a small member, yet boasts great things. See how much wood is kindled by such a small fire!

6 The tongue is such a fire, and the source of iniquity among our members, which defiles the whole body, and sets the course of our life on fire, and is set on fire itself by Gehanna.

7 Every kind of beast, including birds, creeping things, and things in the sea, have been tamed by mankind,

8 but the tongue no man has been able to tame. It is a restless evil, full of deadly poison.

9 With it we bless our Lord and Father, and by it we curse men, who are made after the likeness of God.

10 Out of the same mouth comes forth blessing and cursing. My brethren, it should not be this way.

11 Does a fountain send forth from the same opening sweet water and bitter?

12 My brethren, can a fig tree produce olives, or a vine produce figs? Neither can salt water yield sweet.

The Source of Wisdom

13 Who is wise and understanding among you? Let him show by his good behavior his works in the humility of wisdom.

14 If you have divisions and bitter jealousy in your heart, do not allow them to rise so that you lie against the truth.

15 This wisdom does not come down from above, but is earthly, carnal, demonic.

16 For where there is jealousy and selfish ambition there is confusion, and every evil thing.

17 The wisdom that is from above is first pure, then peaceable, gentle, easy to be entreated, full of mercy and good fruit, does not waver, and is without hypocrisy.

18 The seed whose fruit is righteousness is sown in peace by those who make peace.

The Power of Words

James 3:1-12: Teachers receive stricter judgment because they have the high responsibility of providing spiritual food for the household of the King. In biblical times, to prepare food for the king's household was one of the greatest responsibilities one could have. If we were a head chef at the White House or in the palace of a king, would we not seek to serve the finest food and to hire the very best cooks to prepare it? How much more should teachers be careful about what spiritual food they serve the household of the King of kings?

The Lord stated in Matthew 12:36 that we will be judged by every careless word we speak. "Careless" means to care less.

Teachers above all must be careful, or full of care with their words.

We may have several hundred things wrong with us that need correction, but it is the devil's strategy to wear us out by trying to get us to work on all of them at the same time. Usually the Lord just wants to work on one, or at the most two, knowing that if we have a breakthrough and victory in one area, everything else in our lives will be easier to overcome. The one area most of us should work on is our tongues. If that were brought under the control of the Spirit, our lives would be much easier. It is the tongue that "sets on fire" the course of our lives.

The Source of Wisdom

3:13-18: This is the most concise and illuminating text in The Bible about discernment. We must determine the source of our thoughts before we agree with them or act on them. It is easy to distinguish those that come from above because they lead to peace. Peace will never be known by those who are selfishly ambitious. When we discern selfish ambition in someone's motives, we know that they have not been sent from above.

NOTES

THE EPISTLE OF
JAMES

James 4

The Source of Conflict

1 Where do the wars and conflicts among you come from? Are they not the result of your desires being at war with your members?

2 You lust, and do not have, so you covet, which drives men to murder. Because you cannot obtain you fight and war with one another. You do not have because you do not ask.

3 When you ask you do not receive because you ask with wrong motives, so that you can spend what you receive on your lusts.

4 You adulteresses! Do you not understand that friendship with the world is hostility toward God? Therefore whoever desires to be a friend of the world makes himself an enemy of God.

5 Do you think that the Scripture speaks in vain? Is the Spirit that He gave to dwell in us for lust or envying?

Walking in His Grace

6 But He gives greater grace, and because of this the Scripture says, "God resists the proud, but gives grace to the humble" (see Proverbs 3:34).

7 Therefore subject yourselves to God, resist the devil, and he will flee from you.

8 Draw near to God, and He will draw near to you. Cleanse your hands, you sinners, and purify your hearts you double-minded.

9   Be afflicted, and mourn, and weep. Let your laughter be turned to mourning, and your mirth to heaviness.

10 Humble yourselves in the sight of the Lord, and He will exalt you.

Arrogant Behavior

11 Do not speak against another, brethren. He that speaks against a brother, or judges his brother, speaks against the law, and judges the law. If you are a judge of the law, you are not a doer of the law, but a judge.

12 Only One is the Lawgiver and Judge–He who is able to save and to destroy. Who are you that you judge your neighbor?

13 Consider this, those of you who say, "Today or tomorrow we will go into this city, and spend a year there, and trade, and make a profit."

14 You do not know what tomorrow will bring. What is your life? For your life is but a vapor that appears for a short time, and then vanishes away.

15 For this reason you should say, "If the Lord wills, we will both live, and do this or that."

16 Now you glory in your boasting, which is evil.

17 Therefore, to him that knows to do good and does not do it, it is sin to him.

The Source of Conflict

James 4:1-5: The word translated "earnestly desire" the gifts of the Spirit in I Corinthians 14:1 is the same word for lust. The way we counter lust for the things of the world is to use this passion to seek the things of the Spirit.

We are called to love the world because God does, which is why He sent His Son. However, we are not to love the things of this world or its ways. We are not to be friends with the world, because friends have common interests, and we are not to have the same interests as those who are in the world. One of the ways we can determine if we truly are "seeking first the

kingdom" is the degree to which we spend our time and effort seeking the kingdom and how much time we spend seeking the things of this world.

Walking in His Grace

4:6-10: There is no earthly fortune, power, position, or fame that is as valuable as the grace of God. As one great seeker of God said, "One moment of the favor of God is worth a lifetime of effort." When we grasp that God resists the proud, but gives His grace to the humble, we would be constantly seeking ways to humble ourselves, make ourselves look smaller and less important, rather than bigger and more important. That is the path to the most fulfilling life we can have—one filled with the grace and favor of the Lord. It is also a life with the great freedom of not having to uphold a façade.

We are told to humble ourselves; nowhere does it say God will humble us. However, it does say that if we will do this, He will exalt us at the proper time. Therefore, it is our place to humble ourselves and God's place to do the exalting. If we try to do His job, He will do ours.

Arrogant Behavior

4:11-17: After the exhortation to humble ourselves to seek God's grace, James addresses the highest form of pride—judging and criticizing others. By criticizing someone else, we are considering ourselves to be superior to them. Likewise, if we criticize someone else's children, we are really criticizing the parents. If we criticize God's children, we are saying that we do not approve of the way He is raising them. If we criticize the church, we are saying that we do not approve of God's workmanship, and we are presenting ourselves as being superior. How much more of God's grace would there be in the church if we could control our tongues and overcome this one problem?

Have you ever noticed that most critical people have never really accomplished anything significant themselves? There is a saying that goes, "Any jackass can kick a barn down, but it takes a skillful carpenter to build one." Critical people are not only lacking in God's grace because of their pride, but no one likes to be around a critical person, and you are not a leader if someone isn't following you.

NOTES

The Epistle of
JAMES
James 5

Unrighteous Riches

1 Come now, you rich, weep and groan for the miseries that are coming upon you.

2 Your riches are corrupted, and your garments are moth-eaten.

3 Your gold and your silver are corroding, and their rust will be a testimony against you, and will consume your flesh like fire. You have hoarded your treasure in the last days.

4 See, the wages of the laborers who mowed your fields that you held back by fraud, cries out, and the cries of those who reaped have reached the ears of the Lord of Sabbath.

5 You have lived delicately on the earth, and taken your pleasure. You have fattened your hearts in a day of slaughter.

6 You have condemned and killed the righteous, who do not resist you.

Patience in Sowing

7 Be patient therefore, brethren, until the coming of the Lord. Behold, the farmer waits for the precious fruit of the earth, being patient with it, until it receives the early and latter rain.

8 You also be patient. Strengthen your hearts, for the coming of the Lord is at hand.

9 Brethren, do not complain against one another, so that you will not be judged. Behold, the Judge is standing at the door.

10 For an example take the suffering and patience of the prophets who spoke in the name of the Lord.

11 See how we call them blessed that endured. You have heard of the patience of Job, and have seen the result of the Lord's dealing in this matter, how the Lord is full of compassion, and is merciful.

Honoring Our Word

12 In all things, brethren, do not swear, neither by heaven, nor the earth, nor by any other oath. Let your yes mean yes, and your no mean no, so that you do not come under judgment.

Faith Heals

13 Is anyone among you suffering? Let him pray. Is anyone cheerful? Let him sing praises.

14 Is anyone among you sick? Let him call for the elders of the church, and let them pray over him, anointing him with oil in the name of the Lord.

15 The prayer of faith will save him that is sick, and the Lord will raise him up, and if he has committed sins, they shall be forgiven him.

Fervent, Righteous Prayer

16 Therefore confess your sins to one another, and pray for one another so that you may be healed. The prayer of a righteous man will accomplish much.

17 Elijah was a man of like passions as us, and he prayed fervently that it might not rain, and it did not rain on the earth for three and a half years.

18 He prayed again and the heaven gave rain, and the earth brought forth her fruit.

19 My brethren, if any among you strays from the truth, and one converts him,

20 let him know that he who converts a sinner from the error of his way will save a soul from death, and shall cover a multitude of sins.

Unrighteous Riches

James 5:1-6: This is not a condemnation of the wealthy, but of the wealthy who defraud their workers. That is stealing. It is "withholding what is justly due" that the Word is clear "will result only in poverty" (see Proverbs 11:24). This is why there are always times of great transfers of wealth in which the wealthy, who have not been righteous, get to learn how the rest of the people live.

Patience in Sowing

5:7-11: Patience is the demonstration of faith. We are told to be imitators of those who "through faith and patience inherit the promises" (see Hebrews 6:12). We have had a huge "faith movement" in modern Christianity, but why has there not been a "patience movement?" When we leave out half of an ingredient, how good can we expect the product to be? Could this be why so many who presume to have faith still do not get results? Patience is actually one of the greatest demonstrations of true faith, because true faith in God is faith in God, not just an outcome.

Honoring Our Word

5:12: One of the most basic characteristics of the nature of God is that His word is true. If we are going to be His disciples, becoming like Him and His representatives on the earth, our word must also be trustworthy.

Faith Heals

5:13-15: Faith for healing is basic to our faith for salvation. These were both purchased for us by the atonement of Jesus on the cross. Just as Jesus healed everywhere He went when He walked the earth, He is the same today as He was then. He still wants to heal the sick.

James wrote that if a sick person has committed sin, it will be forgiven him, which implies that some sickness can be the result of sin. However, this does not imply that all sickness is the result of sin.

Fervent, Righteous Prayer

5:16-20: Here we are told that the prayer of a righteous person will accomplish much. We are then given the example of Elijah who had passions like we do. We are not righteous because we are perfect, but because we have faith in God, His atonement, and His redemption. Even the most righteous may still have passions, but as we are told in Proverbs 24:16, "The righteous man falls seven times and rises yet again." Even the righteous may fall, but they will not stay down. They rise again and keep pressing on.

NOTES

The Epistle of James
Proper Names and Definitions

Abraham: father of a multitude, exalted father

Christ: anointed

Elijah: heifer, chariot, round, Yah is God

Isaac: laughter, he shall laugh, mockery

James: one who supplants, undermines, heel-catcher, he whom God protects

Jesus: Savior, Deliverer, Yahweh is salvation

Lord of Sabaoth: Lord of armies

Rahab: large, extended name of a woman, proud, quarrelsome applied to Egypt, storm, act stormily, boisterous, arrogant, sea monster, strength, broad/breadth